# Our Global Village

# Mexico

By: Nancy Klepper

Illustrated By: Larry Nolte

Milliken Publishing Co.　　　St. Louis, Missouri　　　Copyright © 1990

To Adam, my son, and to the curiosity in all children. – N.K.

Milliken Publishing Company
1100 Research Blvd., St. Louis, Missouri 63132

Edited by: Carole E. Garrett
Cover Design by: Larry Nolte

ISBN 1-55863-154-2

# Table of Contents

# A Multicultural Experience

*Our Global Village* hopes to share ideas, hands-on activities, and resources from other cultures which will lead you, your students, and their families in different experiences. Our heritage is indeed multicultural. Learning how others live, think, and react is becoming more important. The earth is a global village, and each of us is quickly affected by events, styles, disasters, and ideas from far away. Old barriers of mountains and oceans are disappearing with fax machines and airplanes. It is important to help young children learn about and value the diversity in the world around them. Fortunate is the child who has the opportunity to be with people who speak different languages, who eat different foods, and whose skins are different colors. This child will come to appreciate the fascinating differences between people in the world while learning that people are much the same. We hope this resource series will help to create a multicultural community in your classroom as you learn and share different languages, customs, and celebrations.

# Mexico

Many countries in the Western Hemisphere have been greatly influenced by this Spanish-speaking country. When we share the richness and diversity of the Mexican culture with children, we enable them to appreciate an important part of our heritage, and we strengthen their interest in cultural and ethnic pluralism.

**Area**–761,001 square miles.

**Capital**–Mexico City. Its current population of 13,500,000 makes Mexico City one of the largest cities in the world.

**Population**–81,098,000 (estimate as of 1986 census)

**Race**–The peoples of Mexico are descendants of both the Spanish settlers and the indigenous populations.

**Religion**–Predominately Roman Catholic with an integration of Indian religions.

**Language**–Mexico is the largest Spanish-speaking country in the world. Spanish is the official language. Varieties of Indian languages are also spoken.

**Currency**–The peso. 1 peso = 100 centavos (cents).

## Natural Environment

Mexico is a country of great geographical diversity. The Sierra Madre are an extension of the Rocky Mountains of the United States. They reach more than halfway to the southern tip of Mexico. These mountainous ranges reach elevations of more than 6,000 feet, forming highlands of the Tierra Fria (cold land). The Central Plateau and parts of the highlands that are between 3,000 and 6,000 feet in elevation are known as the Tierra Templada (temperate lands). The lowland areas of the Tierra Caliente (hot lands) border the Pacific Ocean and the Gulf of Mexico.

The agricultural products of Mexico reflect the country's climatic zones and altitudes. For example, cotton, sugar cane, and tropical fruits such as papayas and mangoes are grown in the lowlands. Coffee and maize (corn) are grown in cooler climates at higher altitudes.

## The Flag of Mexico

The Mexican flag has three vertical stripes consisting of green (which stands for independence), white (religion), and red (union). The coat of arms, located in the center of the white stripe, is based on an ancient Aztec prophecy. In about 1325, when the Aztecs were looking for a secure place to build their capital, they sighted an eagle perched on a cactus on an island in a lake. In its talons, the bird held a snake. The leaders of the tribe took this as a good omen. They named their great city, Tenochtitlan. Their city was destroyed by the Spanish conqueror, Cortes, and their culture eventually collapsed. Out of the ruins emerged Mexico City, which took its name from the Mexican tribe of the Aztec Nation.

## In Your Classroom:

Explain the legend of the Aztec's search for the eagle-serpent. Display the flag of Mexico with its emblem.

Have the children compare their own state flag to the flag of Mexico. Ask if they know the origins of the coat of arms on their state flag.

Have the children design a coat of arms for their family, incorporating ideas about the family, its members, where they live, and what they do.

## A Key to Spanish Pronunciation

Say *a* as in *father*          The *h* is never sounded.
Say *e* as in *met*.           Both *j* and *x* are sounded like *h*
Say *i* as in the *e* in *me*.   Say *ll* like a *y* in *you*.
Say *o* as in *go*.            Say *n* like the *ny* in *canyon*.

# A History of Mexico

## Pre-Columbian Peoples

The Indian civilizations of Mexico, before the arrival of the Europeans in 1519, were cultures of complex organization, sophisticated architecture, and great wealth. Outstanding craftsmanship prevailed in the temples, decorated with beautiful murals and sculptures. The Olmecs (1200 B.C.) shaped beautiful carvings of human figures made of jade. Other groups in Mexico also had wide ranging influence on Mexican culture.

The Teotihuacan people were not only artistically and scientifically sophisticated, but were responsible for building two extraordinary and breathtakingly large pyramids, one to the sun and the other to the moon. The Teotihuacans also developed agricultural products such as chocolate and corn that were later introduced in Europe.

The Mayans were known as the Mexican Greeks as they built perfectly proportioned and lavishly decorated buildings. The Aztecs are equally well-known for their scientific, artistic, and astronomical contributions.

## The Conquering of Mexico

When the Spanish landed on Mexico in 1519, the Aztec emperor, Montezuma, sent messengers with welcoming gifts of precious stones, gold, and silver. This was probably Montezuma's greatest mistake, for as soon as the Spanish saw the beautiful gifts, they decided to conquer the Aztecs and plunder their wealth.

To reach the great Aztec city, Cortes and his men had to journey over high mountains and through thick jungles. They finally succeeded and laid siege to Tenochtitlan. For three months, the Indians fought the Spanish, but they finally fell on August 31, 1521. The great emperor, Montezuma, was killed in 1520. Cortes then succeeded in making the Aztec homeland a Spanish province.

The conquest was a horrible time for the Indians of Mexico. Cortes and the Spanish conquerors had little respect for the Indian civilization and the lives of Indians. They killed people mercilessly and destroyed villages and cities.

## Mayan Math

The Pre-Columbian Indians of Mexico had elaborate mathmatical systems.  The Mayans, for example, had an interesting way of representing numbers.

The symbol for 1 was a dot:  ○

The symbol for 5 was a line:  ▭

This is how the numbers from 1 to 10 were written:

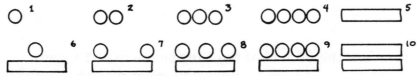

## Spanish Numbers

uno - one
dos - two
tres - three
cuatro - four
cinco - five
seis - six
siete - seven
ocho - eight
nueve - nine
diez - ten

## In Your Classroom:

Teach the children to write the numbers from 1 to 10 using Mayan symbols and work simple math problems.

Take the children to the Pre-Columbian section of the local art museum and look for art that incorporates mathematical symbols.

Teach the children to count in Spanish.  Use Spanish numbers in oral arithmetic activities and games.

# Daily Life

Mexico is a country of great diversity and contrast. Life-styles vary according to regions, rural and urban environment, and economic levels. The extended family is one characteristic of Mexican life that transcends these differences. In extended families, two or three generations live together under the same roof. It is not uncommon to find grandparents, aunts and uncles, and other relatives living together in a family unit. Godparents are also included in the family structure, although they may not live in the same abode. The traditional Mexican family is tight-knit, and family members feel a great affection and loyalty for one another. They often work, socialize, and worship together.

Many houses in Mexico are built around a patio and have no outside garden. These homes are built of bricks with large rooms, high ceilings, and tiled floors. Rooms open onto the patio which usually has pots of flowers, trees, and sometimes fountains. In the countryside, people's homes are often built of adobe brick and are surrounded by fields. Colorful murals depicting life in Mexico are found decorating buildings and homes throughout the country.

In Mexico, a child's last name is a combination of both the father's last name and the mother's maiden name. This Spanish custom identifies a child with the two families to which he belongs. For example, if a child whose first name is Jose has a father named Roberto Garcia and a mother named, before marriage, Maria Marcos, the child is called Jose Garcia Marcos.

## Spanish Words for Family Members

padres - parents
madre - mother
tio - uncle
hija - daughter
hijo - son
padre - father

primo - cousin
abuela - grandmother
abuelo - grandfather
hermana - sister
hermano - brother
padrinos - godparents

## Common Mexican First Names - pronunciation and English equivalent:

Alicia - Alice
Ana - Anna
Andres - Andrew

Antonio - Anthony
Carlos - Charles
Diego - James

Juan - John
Luisa - Louise
Maria - Mary

## Everyday Expressions

hola - hello
buenos dias - good day
gracias - thank you
por favor - please
adios - goodbye

¿Como te llamas? - What is your name?
¿Quantos años tienes? - How old are you?
¿Como estas? - How are you?
  Muy bien gracias. - I am fine.

## In Your Classroom:

Have the children share information about their family members. Have them compare their family structures with a typical Mexican family.

Find pictures of extended families and display them with pictures of the children's families. Label the persons in the pictures with words describing their relationships, using Spanish vocabulary words.

Have the children combine their mother's family name with their father's name to produce the name they would have if they were Mexican.

Invite a Spanish speaker to your classroom. Children are interested in learning Spanish words. It is important that they be exposed to persons who speak Spanish.

Translate your students' names into Spanish. Have the children learn and practice their Spanish names.

Place a Spanish/English dictionary in your classroom and allow the children to find the Spanish equivalent for words describing articles in the room such as clothing and food.

## The Marketplace

The market has been a basic economic institution since the time of early Indian societies. The Aztec word for market, tianguis, is still used in Mexico today. The "Aztecas" and other groups used both barter and articles that substituted for money, including cocoa beans, pieces of tin, and feathers.

The market is important today, particularly for small farmers, agricultural workers, artisans, traders, and small businesspeople. In the market you'll find the weaving, pottery, and folk art of the past mixed with the plastic toys, radios, and blue jeans of today. The market contains a bewildering variety of goods—everything from blankets, goat milk, and cheese to live chickens, eggs, fruits, and vegetables.

Fixed prices are rare. Bargaining is the normal way of buying everything in the market. Sellers typically set prices higher than they expect to receive, sometimes as much as 50% higher. Buyers initially offer to pay a price much lower than they expect to pay. Sellers and buyers offer and counter-offer numerous times. When they reach an agreement and both are satisfied, the item is sold.

In small towns and villages, markets are held on certain days of the week, perhaps over one or two days. The market is usually held in the town's main plaza or square. Market days are festive occasions with much talking, storytelling, and socializing among people in the market. On market day, a great variety of dress is on display. The Indians often wear traditional dress—the women wear long, colorful skirts and beautifully embroidered shirts. Mothers wear colorful shawls, called rebozas, which they use to carry their babies on their backs. Men wear white cotton pants and shirts along with ponchos, sombreros, and huaraches (sandals).

Markets in larger cities are open seven days a week. They are much larger and they contain a wider variety of specialized goods. Large city markets are often housed in special buildings constructed just for this purpose.

## In Your Classroom:

Create a marketplace in your classroom for ongoing play and dramatization. Furnish the market with foods, baskets, and Mexican artifacts. Have the children make folk art and handicrafts to place in the market.

Hold a market day. Let the children make their own traditional costumes to wear on this day.

Visit open markets or farmer's markets in your own community. Observe the differences between these markets and Mexican markets.

Visit a local Mexican grocery store.

Use the topic of the market to introduce economic concepts such as barter, money, bargaining, and work. Have the children incorporate these concepts into play and dramatization.

Compare supermarkets and department stores with traditional markets.

# Foods

## Things to Make and Taste

Mexican foods and cooking methods have been greatly influenced by the Indian and Spanish cultures. The Indians introduced vanilla, corn, chocolate, sweet potatoes, tomatoes, papayas, chilies, avocados, and pineapples.

A wonderful diversity of foods is found throughout Mexico. Each region has its own specialities. Not all Mexican food is spicy, and it is much more varied than tacos, enchiladas, and refried beans (refritos). However, meat and vegetables are expensive, and many people have daily diets of beans, tortillas, and chili peppers.

Mexicans begin their day with breakfast (desayuno), frequently with chocolate or cafe con leche (milk and coffee). A heartier second breakfast (almuerzo) is eaten later in the morning. It might include fruit and fruit juices, beans, and tortillas. The main meal of the day (the comida) takes place anytime between 2:00 p.m. and 5:30 p.m. There is a light meal at night (the merienda) which is eaten by children in early evening and by adults as late as 9:00 p.m. The Cena is a dinner for a special occasion, eaten very late.

## Tortillas

*Taco* means *snack*. In Mexico, tacos are made from any available food, wrapped in a soft tortilla. The tortilla is folded in half and rolled around the filling. To make tortillas, corn is first well-soaked in jars of limewater. Then the women grind the wet, softened kernels on a flat stone called a metate (meh TAH tay). They add a little water from time to time to keep the corn wet. The corn is ground until it is a smooth, doughy mass. Bits of this masa (HAH sah) are then patted into round, thin cakes and toasted

Ingredients:
4 cups of flour
3/4 cup hot water - add more if needed
1 tsp. salt
1 cup shortening

Mix flour, salt, and shortening. Add hot water a little at a time. Mix until firm and let stand. Take heaping tablespoon size quantities to make rounds (testables) by rolling with a rolling pin. Cook on a hot griddle with low flame. Serve as bread with a meal or spread with butter or margarine.

## Soup (Sopas)

Ordinary soup is referred to as caldo or "wet" soup whereas sopas or "dry" soup is thicker and contains rice. The following sopa recipe can be used as a first course.

Ingredients:

1 cup white rice
3 cloves garlic (or to taste)
1 tomato
1 onion
salad oil
1 tsp. powdered chicken soup or bullion cube

Chop garlic. Combine tomato and onion in a blender until liquified. Put rice and oil in the sauce pan and brown. When half-done, add the garlic and cook until golden brown. Add tomato and onion mixture, chicken soup powder, and water to cover. Cover pan and cook slowly, adding water if necessary, until done (takes about 45 minutes).

## Chocolate

Chocolate originated with the early Indians of Mexico, but it was enjoyed only by the most important people. Today it is widely consumed. Sometimes chocolate is flavored with honey or vanilla. Chocolate is traditionally mixed with a wooden spoon or paddle.

Mexican children recite the following chant as they mix their chocolate.

Uno - dos - tres - cho
Uno - dos - tres - co
Uno - dos - tres - la
Uno - dos - tres - te
Cho - co - la - te
Bate - bate
cho - co - la - te.

BATÉ - BATÉ
CHO · CO · LATÉ

9

## Spanish Words for Food and Drink

agua - water
leche - milk
chocolate - chocolate
tortilla - tortilla
sopa, caldo - soup
pan - bread
papa - potato
pollo - chicken
frijole - bean
tomate - tomato
naranja - orange
platano - banana
duranzno - peach
fresa - strawberry
manzana - apple
dulce - candy
helado - ice cream

## In Your Classroom:

Have the children mix chocolate into milk with wooden spoons or wire wisks and chant the chocolate song as they mix.

Prepare a Mexican dinner at school. Invite parents to participate.

Have the children make soup after reading *Mexicalai Soup* (see Additional Resources).

Visit a local Mexican restaurant or a tortilla factory.

# Creative Arts
### Music, Dance, Arts

## Music

Music is an integral part of Mexican life, particularly at festivals. Guitars, violins, marimbas, and trumpets are played by strolling bands, dressed in fancy suits.

The following song, "Buenos Dias," is sung by Mexican children (to the tune of "Happy Birthday").

| | |
|---|---|
| Buenos dias a ustedes, | Good morning to you, |
| Buenos dias a ustedes, | Good morning to you, |
| Buenos dias, Buenos dias, | Good morning, good morning, |
| Buenos dias a ustedes. | Good morning to you. |

## Dance

Each region of Mexico has dances typical of the area. These dances are always performed at festivals. The best known of these, the Mexican Hat Dance, is the national dance of Mexico.

The Mexican Hat Dance is easy to learn. Have the children form a large circle or circles. Children put one heel into the circle at a time, alternating feet with the rhythm of the music. Everyone then dances to the right around the circle until the music changes when they turn and dance in a circle to the left. Repeat the heel movements. Then everyone joins hands and dances to the center of the circle, raising joined hands high. Then dance back, forming a big circle again, bend low. Repeat the whole sequence several times.

# Costumes

Traditional costumes are worn at festivals throughout Mexico and reflect the different cultures of each region of the country. Children can make their own costumes from pieces of unbleached cotton fabric or sets of old sheets. These can be decorated with markers or paints. The following are common items of clothing.

Rebozos are colorful shawls worn by girls and women over their heads and shoulders.

Serapes are small blankets worn over the shoulder by boys and men.

Ponchos are worn by children and adults as a jacket or wrap. They are blankets with an opening in the middle for the head.

Poblana are long, full skirts worn by women and girls on festive occasions. Poblana are considered the national folk dress and are always worn for the Hat Dance. Children can use colored fabric or crepe paper to make these red or green skirts. Decorations of beads or glitter can be glued in designs of the children's choosing. A short-sleeved white shirt decorated with red and green ribbon streamers completes the costume.

Charro suits are worn on festive occasions by musicians as well as by men and boys. The charro includes a boleros (short jacket), trousers, white shirt, and a flowing, red bow for a tie. Boots, a wide leather belt, serape, sombrero (wide brimmed hat), and huaraches (leather sandals) complete the outfit.

Waist sashes can be worn by girls and boys. Children can design their own from a 3" x 36" piece of fabric.

## Jewelry

Colorful clay beads can be made from a baking soda and cornstarch clay and colored with food coloring. These can be strung on pipe cleaners.

## Masks

Masks are used in many Mexican celebrations. The Cora Indians of the Sierra Madre celebrate fiestas by wearing masks and painting their bodies. Masks are constructed of paper mache and made in the image of mythical, wild beasts with fierce and exaggerated expressions, bulging eyes, extended chins, and enlarged noses. Bright colors add to the fantastic appearance of these masks. Children can make their own masks from a great variety of materials including paper bags, paper plates, screen, and paper-mache.

## Decorations

Tissue paper flowers are a popular Mexican handcraft and are an easy-to-make fiesta decoration.

1. Take about six sheets of tissue paper and fold like a paper fan.
2. Cut the folded paper in half (this will make two flowers).
3. Take each half of the paper, still folded, and trim the ends into a broad point.
4. Bend a florist wire or garbage-bag tie around the center of each folded strip of paper.
5. Lift each layer of the folded paper until it forms a circular-shaped flower.
6. Tape the ends of the paper together so that the flower remains open.

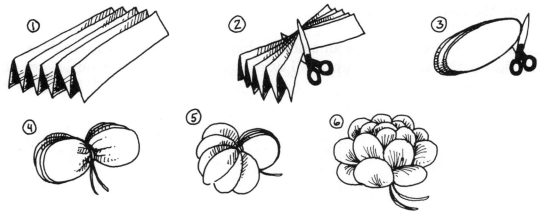

## Folk Art

Ojo de dios is a folk art object. The name comes from an Indian word for "god's eye." It is the symbol of power and is believed to bring wishes for good health, fortune, and a long life. Parents believe that small ojos worn in their children's hair will ward off spells and evil spirits.

Colors of the ojo de dios have special meaning since certain gods have colors they favor. Shades of blue and turquoise are the choice of the rain god, green pleases the god of fertility, while yellow is worn for the sun god. Ojos de dios are not just sticks and yarn, but have a history and meaning. Even today they are bright, cheerful wishes of good-will.

The god's eye design is usually composed of two crossed sticks, wrapped with colorful yarns from the center outward in concentric rows to form a diamond pattern. This is done by going from arm to arm and around each in turn. The center can be made of black to form a pupil for the eye, and the brightest color surrounds the black to call attention to the center. Sometimes an open space is left in the center "to see through."

Tie two sticks of about equal length together in their centers at right angles to each other. Tie one end of the colored yarn at the center of the crossed sticks. Weave the yarn on the sticks by going over one stick and under the next stick repeatedly.

## Paper Making

In ancient Mexico, paper was used in religious ceremonies as offerings to the gods and as ornaments for idols in the temples and palaces on feast days. Bark paper was used to make books written in hieroglyphics.

Paper making still survives among Indians in remote places in Mexico. The men gather the inner bark from certain trees in the spring just before the rainy season begins, and the women make the paper with a process that is essentially the same as the one used by the Aztecs.

The images used in the paintings include double-headed mythical birds catching squirming snakes with their beaks, graceful deer and cock chickens, wildflowers and lizard-like creatures.

Materials:

Brown paper bags
Water colors or tempera paints
Black felt-tip markers
Paint brushes

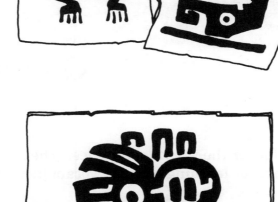

Directions:

1. Cut rectangular panels, 8"x10",
   from the paper bags, big enough
   for children to work with.
2. Soak the paper in water;
   crumble and wring until damp
   dry.
3. Place paper on a smooth surface
   and brush with watered-down
   black tempera.  Set the
   paper in the sun to dry.

4. Draw designs on the paper and paint with regular or florescent tempera.
5. Outline the designs with the black felt-tip marker.

## In Your Classroom:

Have children make some of the art projects described above and sell them on "Market
Day."

Display art objects in the classroom and invite parents to a "Mexican art showing."

# Games

Children all over the world love games.  The games of Mexico can be wonderful opportunities for learning Spanish vocabulary and basic math skills.

## Pinata

The best known festival game and decoration is the pinata.   The pinata is of Spanish origin and was brought to Mexico more than 400 years ago.  Traditional pinatas are made from paper-mache, layers of crepe paper, or earthen jars. They are elaborately decorated and filled with many small toys and foods such as peanuts and candy.

Children can make a pinata from a lightweight cardboard box or shopping bag.  Fill the pinata with candies, fruit, or small toys.  Wrap each item individually.  Decorate the pinata with crepe paper streamers.  Suspend it by a rope at a height just above arm's reach of those who will play the game.  The ceiling or a tree limb will do well.  It is important that the rope be strung through a hook, eye screw, or pulley so that the pinata can be moved up and down by an adult.

To play the pinata game, blindfolded children take turns trying to break the pinata with a decorated broom stick (allow for plenty of swinging space). The adult controlling the rope can move the pinata up and down, making this difficult to do.  After three swings, another child takes a turn.  Make the game more interesting by giving the pinata a big swing from time to time or by spinning the child before she tries to hit the pinata.  The game ends when the pinata is broken.  At this point, all children scramble for the gifts that litter the floor.

Children may recite the following poem during the pinata activity:

See the colored paper,
tied around an earthen jar;
Pinata filled with candy,
and toys from the bazaar;
It hangs above your head,
you take a stick to break it;
And scramble for the candy,
before the others take it.

## Dominoes

Dominoes is a popular game with people of all ages, and it is a good math learning game for children. The game can be adapted to groups of differing ages and abilities and used for developing counting, matching, memory, and strategy skills. Use Spanish number-vocabulary while playing the game (see page 4).

## Corrida de Toros (The Bullfight)

Bullfighting is an important national pastime in Mexico, and it is considered an art form. Children can portray a bullfight, taking roles of the el toro (bull), and the matador and his assistants, the picadores, and the banderilleros. The spectators cheer "ole" as the bull (carefully) charges the matador's cape and the assistants help the matador.

## Colores (Colors)

This game teaches the Spanish names for colors.
1. Choose one leader, one devil, and one angel, then secretly assign individual colors to each member of the rest of the group by giving them different colored ribbons or slips of paper which they keep hidden.
2. Mark a safe area some distance from the group.
3. Dialogue:
    Leader: What do you want?
    Devil: A ribbon.
    Leader: What color?
    Devil: (names a color)

4. The child who has been assigned the color named by the Devil runs from the leader to the safe area.
5. The Devil tries to catch the runner before she reaches the safe area. If the runner is caught, the runner joins the Devil and becomes his helper.
6. Next, the Angel repeats the Devil's dialogue, answering the leader and trying to catch a runner.
7. The Devil and the Angel take turns. The game is over when all colors have been captured. Whoever has captured the largest number of colors is the winner.

## Spanish Words for Colors

negro - black
rojo - red
azul - blue
rosado - pink
marron - brown

blanco - white
verde - green
amarillo - yellow
morado - purple
naranja - orange

# Festivals and Celebrations

## Fiesta

The best known Mexican celebration is the fiesta. It is always fiesta time somewhere in Mexico. Each town and village has its own patron saint with an annual fiesta. There are also Mexican fiestas that are not religious, including such national and civic holidays as El Grito, or Independence Day. Traditional costumes, music, songs, dances, parades, foods, rodeos, bullfights and fireworks are common to most fiestas. Celebrate a fiesta in your classroom. Sing, dance, and share foods.

## Name Day

Religion plays an important role in the daily lives of most Mexicans. Parents tradition-ally give their child the name of at least one saint. A child is often given the name of the saint whose day is closest to the day on which he or she is born. In fact, it is the custom to attach more importance to one's saint's day than to one's birthday. A birth-day is acknowledged with small, inexpensive gifts, whereas one's saint's day is the occasion for a festive gathering of friends and family. A special way of observing a person's saint's day is to bring a gallo (serenade) to the one being honored. A mariachi band (strolling musicians) goes to the person's house and plays outside while friends sing the traditional song for this occasion, "Las Manitas," "The Little Morning Song."

## Los Posadas (The Lodging), December 16-24

Christmas in Mexico begins on December 16 with the Posada Procession. A procession is held each night until Christmas. Los Posadas commemorate the nine-day journey of Mary and Joseph to Bethlehem, during which they were refused lodging. Each night's procession is led by two children rep-resenting Mary and Joseph, holding figures of the Christ Child. The procession stops at houses along the way.  The travelers sing a song, asking for shelter, only to be answered by the people in the house to "Go away! There is no room in this inn!"  The singing is repeated each night, but on the last night, Christmas Eve, the answering song is, "They may sleep in the stable."  Then the door opens and the people file into the house for a celebration with food and music.  A pinata game is a highlight of the party for children.

Traditionally, gifts are not exchanged until January 6 on the Day of the Kings, or Epiphany.  Children place their shoes at the entrance to the front door on the eve of Epiphany.  They awaken the next morning to find their shoes filled with small toys, and candy.  Read *Nine Days to Christmas* to the children (see Additional Resources).  Hold a pinata party in your classroom.

## Los Dias de los Muertos (The Days of the Dead), November 1 and 2

Los Dias de los Muertos, sometimes called All Souls Day, is an important Mexican holiday.  This two-day festival is held on November 1 and 2 and commemorates the spirits of deceased loved ones.  It is a special family day, and is a celebration to receive the returning spirits.  It is a joyous celebration similar to Halloween.

By mid-October, bakeries are hard at work, creating special breads and buns in the form of animals and people.  Candies are made in the shape of skulls and are decorated with bright icing.  Dulce de calabaza (pumpkin candy), pepitas (pumpkin seeds), and pan de muerto (bread of the dead) are some of the foods served.  Special toys, usually skeletons, are made in all forms–puppets, masks, etc.

Parades with costumed skeletons cavort through the streets.  People travel from house to house, singing songs and celebrating the dead.  At each house, after the singing is over, food is offered to the singers.

## In Your Classroom:

Make an El Esqueleto Que Canto (Singing Skeleton).  Singing, swinging skeletons are a common sight during the Days of the Dead.  Skeletons are portrayed engaged in all types of daily activity.

Have the children construct a skeleton puppet.  They can decorate the puppet, for example, with a hat and guitar.

Learn more about the origins of Halloween.  Compare traditional Halloween foods and activities with those of Mexican Days of The Dead.

# Additional Resources

## Books for Children

Aardema, Verna. *The Riddle of the Drum*. Four Winds, 1979. A Mexican version of an old Spanish tale, written with rhyming chants.

Aliki. *Corn is Maize: The Gift of the Indians*. Thomas Y. Crowell Co., 1976. The author tells the story of corn in this fascinating and informative science book.

Behrens, June. *Fiesta! Ethnic Traditional Holidays*. Children's Press, 1978.

Ets, M. H., and A. Labastida. *Nine Days to Christmas*. Viking Press, 1959. A gentle story of a loving, modern Mexican family.

Franco, Ernesto. *The Ball Game*. Indian Traditional Series. Voluntad Publications, 7800 Shoal Creek, Blvd., Austin, TX 78757.

Glubok, Shirley. *The Art of Ancient Mexico*. Harper & Row Publishers, 1968. Photographs of Mexican works of art open an opportunity to view the variety of Indian cultures that flourished before the Spanish invasion.

Hitte, K. and W. Hayes. *Mexicalai Soup*. Parent's Magazine Press, 1970. Told in rhythmic prose; it's fun for both the reader and for the children who listen.

Kurtycz, M., and A. B. Kobeh. *Tigers and Possums: Animal Legends*. Little, Brown, and Co.,1984. Legends with a traditional Mexican sense of irony and sympathy; good illustrations.

Politi, Leo. *Juanita*. Charles Scribner's Sons, 1948. The story of a birthday party and the colorful Easter blessing of the animals.

Politi, Leo. *Sons of the Swallows*. Charles Scribner's Sons, 1948. A Caldecott Award winner. A story of friendship.

Rohmer, Harriet. *The Legend of Food Mountain*. Children's Book Press, 1982. The creation legend and the importance of preserving the earth's resources. The text is in both English and Spanish.

Somonte, Carlos. *We Live in Mexico*. Bookwright Press, 1985. Interviews and photos with people of all backgrounds showing the Mexican way of life.

## Resources for Teachers

Calvert, Peter. *The Mexicans: How They Live and Work*. Praeger Publishers, 1975.

Casagrande, L., and S. Johnson. *Focus on Mexico: Modern Life in an Ancient Land*. Lerner Publishing Co., 1986. Modern-day Mexico with excellent historic and contemporary photographs.

Cole, A., C. Haas, E. Heller, and B. Weinberger. *Children Are Children Are Children*. Little, Brown and Company, 1978.

Garza-Lubeck, M., and A.M. Salinas. *Mexican Celebrations*. Institute of Latin American Studies, University of Texas, Austin, TX 78712, 1977.

Gibbs, Virginia G., ed. *Latin America: Curriculum Materials for the Middle Grades*. Center for Latin America, University of Wisconsin, Milwaukee, 1985. The section on Mexico has numerous ideas for hands-on activities. A valuable resource for any material on Latin America.

Glab, Edward, Jr., ed. *Latin American Culture Studies*. Institute of Latin American Studies, The University of Texas at Austin, Austin, TX 78712, 1981. Information and materials for teaching Latin American culture.

Gorena, Minerva. *Information and Materials to Teach the Cultural Heritage of the Mexican American Child*. Bilingual Resource Center, 7703 North Lamar, Austin, TX 78752, 1981. An excellent source of background information and material on all aspects of Mexican-American culture.

*Indian Mexico*. Huntsville, Texas: Edal Filmstrips.

Lane, S., and M. Turkovich. *Los Dias De Los Muertos–The Days of the Dead*. Associates in Multicultural and International Education, Chicago, IL, 1989.

Lee, N., and L. Oldham. *Hands -on Heritage: An Experimental Approach to Multicultural Education*. B. L. Winch and Associates, 45 Hitching Post Drive, Rolling Hills Estate, CA 90274, 1978. This action packet contains numerous classroom activities on Mexico for youth.

McNeill, E., et al. *Cultural Awareness for Young Children*. The Learning Tree, Dallas, TX, 1981. A wonderful, hands-on resource with a section on Mexican-American culture.

*Mexican Folk Dances*. BP-211LP, Bowmar Records, 622 Rodier Drive, Glendale, CA 91201. Includes diagrams and instructions for Mexican folk dances.

Milne, Jean. *Fiesta Time in Los Angeles*. Ward Richies, 1975.

Thompson, Kathryn. *Algunos Animales De Latino America*. Institute of Latin American Studies, Office of Outreach Programs, University of Texas, Austin, TX 78712.

# NOTES

# NOTES